D1533461

Grand Canyon National Park South Rim Tour Guide

By Waypoint Tours®

Front Cover - Grand Canyon Sunset from Maricopa Point

Back Cover - The Watchtower at Desert View

Contents

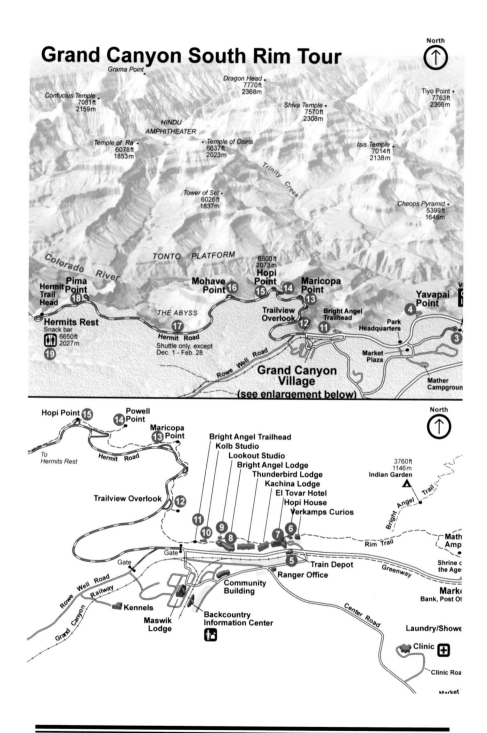

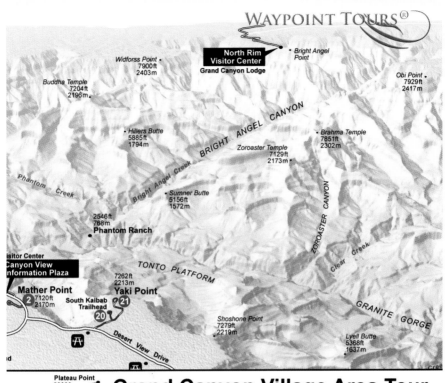

Grand Canyon Village Area Tour

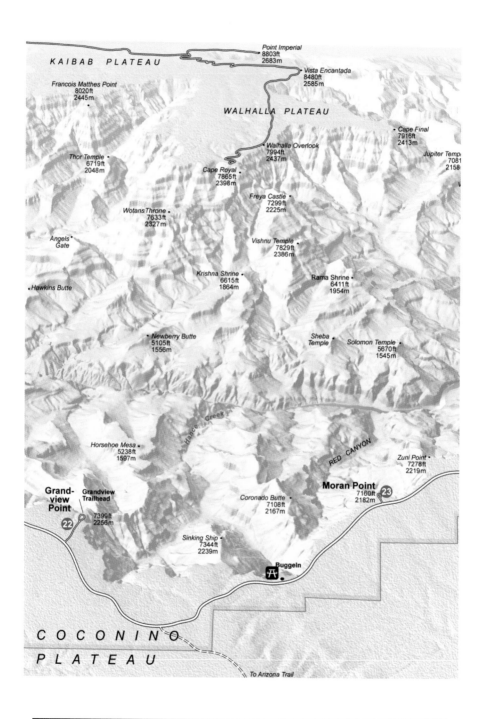

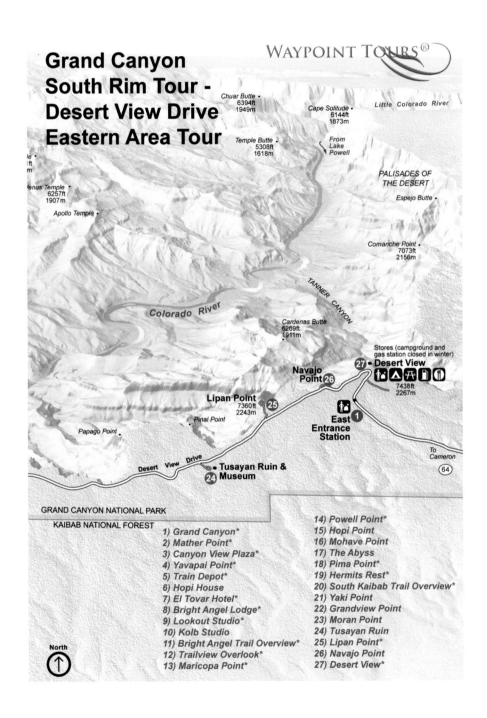

Grand Canyon South Rim Tour - Desert View Drive Eastern Area Tour

WAYPOINT TOURS®

Chuar Butte • 6394ft 1949m

Cape Solitude • 6144ft 1873m

Little Colorado River

Temple Butte • 5308ft 1618m

From Lake Powell

PALISADES OF THE DESERT

Espejo Butte •

Venus Temple • 6257ft 1907m

Apollo Temple •

Comanche Point • 7073ft 2156m

TANNER CANYON

Colorado River

Cardenas Butte 6269ft 1911m

Stores (campground and gas station closed in winter)

Navajo Point 26

27 • **Desert View** 7438ft 2267m

Lipan Point 7360ft 2243m 25

Pinal Point •

East Entrance Station 1

Papago Point •

Desert View Drive

24 **Tusayan Ruin & Museum**

To Cameron

64

GRAND CANYON NATIONAL PARK

KAIBAB NATIONAL FOREST

North

1) Grand Canyon*
2) Mather Point*
3) Canyon View Plaza*
4) Yavapai Point*
5) Train Depot*
6) Hopi House
7) El Tovar Hotel*
8) Bright Angel Lodge*
9) Lookout Studio*
10) Kolb Studio
11) Bright Angel Trail Overview*
12) Trailview Overlook*
13) Maricopa Point*

14) Powell Point*
15) Hopi Point
16) Mohave Point
17) The Abyss
18) Pima Point*
19) Hermits Rest*
20) South Kaibab Trail Overview*
21) Yaki Point
22) Grandview Point
23) Moran Point
24) Tusayan Ruin
25) Lipan Point*
26) Navajo Point
27) Desert View*

1) Grand Canyon South Rim

Welcome to Grand Canyon National Park! As you approach the Grand Canyon, you are crossing the Colorado Plateau, a 130,000 square mile bulge in the earth's surface spanning half of Utah and a good portion of Arizona, New Mexico, and Colorado. Around its edges are the upthrust Rocky Mountains, the stretched-apart Great Basin, the contorted rocks of Arizona's Transition Zone, and ancient volcanoes. Despite all the geologic activity around it, the plateau has managed to stay relatively flat and unfolded, but as a whole, it may have been uplifted nearly two miles.

It is the uplift and the down cutting that have created the canyon. About five to six million years ago, the Colorado River began to carve its way down through the domed region on its way to the sea. Like a knife slicing through a layer cake, the mile-deep river canyon exposed multi-hued layers of time; a geologist's dream come true. However, you don't have to be a geologist to appreciate the canyon's grandeur.

Erosion by wind, water, and gravity not only widened the canyon, it created an amazing variety of towers and spires, ridges and side canyons, shadows and highlights. The rainbow of rock colors is most intense in early morning or late afternoon light. If you are lucky, you will see a storm chase through the canyon casting shadows and mist as it goes.

Sightseers have been coming to view the wonders of the canyon since 1883. Prospectors soon found tourism more profitable than mining and built accommodations for them. One of the earliest visitors was Theodore Roosevelt, a lover of the West's wide-open spaces. He pushed for federal protection and in 1893, the area became a Forest Reserve. In 1908, it received a promotion to National Monument and in 1919, the National Park was authorized by Congress. The most recent upgrade was in 1975 when its boundaries were expanded, doubling its size.

As you enter the park, you'll receive a copy of the park newspaper, *The Guide*, from the National Park Service, which is a great source of information on restaurants, lodging, parking, ranger talks, activities and other guest services within or near the park. It includes maps, hours, prices, and other helpful information.

2) **Mather Point**

Beneath the ponderosa pines, scrub oaks, juniper, and pinyons of the South Rim, the ground is fairly level. No matter how well prepared a visitor is, this first view of the canyon is still a delightful, awesome shock. The plateau comes to an abrupt end as the land falls away into a chasm of jagged cliffs, spires, and buttes for mile after mile. The North Rim is ten miles away but looks even farther - and it is, unless you can fly like the ravens.

Looking north across the canyon, you can see a green oasis where Bright Angel Creek emerges from its side canyon and joins the Colorado River. Phantom Ranch is located there and provides lodging for those who hike or ride mules to the bottom. The deep, narrow cleft where the river flows is called the inner gorge.

The bright orange splashes of rock on the far side are Hakatai shale. The vibrant purple-red-orange colors are a result of oxidation of iron-containing minerals in the rocks. Above it is the Tonto Platform, a relatively level area that, from a distance, has a grayish appearance due to evenly spaced blackbrush.

During the heat of the day, most reptiles, like the kingsnake, whipsnake, and rattlesnake hole up, but lizards, such as chuckwalla, spiny lizards, and collared lizards are more active, and can sometimes be seen doing pushups. Watching from above for a meal are ravens, turkey vultures, red-tailed hawks, golden eagles, and California condors.

To the east of Mather Point is a ridge ending in Yaki Point. The sun rising over Yaki Point is an inspiring sight. In 1914, when Stephen Tyng Mather complained about the way Yosemite and Sequoia National Parks were being managed, the Secretary of the Interior wrote back, "If you don't like the way the national parks are being run, come on down to Washington and run them yourself." So Mather did. A retired millionaire, he and his assistant, Horace Albright, worked to create the National Park Service. Mather became its first director in 1916.

After a long struggle, the Grand Canyon finally became a national park in 1919. As President Theodore Roosevelt said, "Keep this great wonder of nature as it now is. . . You cannot improve on it. The ages have been at work on it, and man can only mar it."

3) Canyon View Information Plaza

The visitor center at Canyon View Information Plaza is a great place to plan your visit. Besides a wonderful bookstore, visitor center, and re-strooms, the plaza has beautiful and helpful displays on trails, plant and animal life, weather, geology, and the many recreational activities in and near the park. You can hike or bike; fly above the canyon or raft through its depths; ride a mule, horse, or train; see a sunrise or a sunset; walk the rim, or trek down into the great rift. A popular exhibit, "Choose Your Views," lets tourists see how the Grand Canyon looks from various points at different times of the day so they can optimize their visit.

Notice the signs along the pathways that identify plants. The re-vegetation staff carefully preserved hundreds of plants during the one and a half years of construction and replanted them. Wildflowers abound during the spring.

One of the first to bloom is wild candytuft. Bright red Indian paintbrush is one of the longest lasting flowers on the rim. Flowers gradually diminish as the hot, dry weather of June approaches, but morning glories and lupines are seen in the plaza area

Evening primroses grow along roadways, and each bloom opens for one summer night of pollinating. The monsoons start in July frequently dumping massive quantities of water in short bursts of afternoon storms. The rain brings summer flowers such as the wide, white petals of the sego lily and the brilliant purple wild geranium.

Also, look closely at the visitor center's construction. It was made with ashes, recycled cars, stone from this construction site, and dis-carded rock. The well-planned energy-efficient design takes advantage of the sun for warming and breezes for cool-ing.

4) Yavapai Point

Yavapai Observation Station has a 180-degree panorama. From this point that projects far out into the canyon, you can fully appreciate the true shape, depth, width, and length of the Grand Canyon. It is also a great place to go when it rains; through the large windows you can watch the storm as it moves through the canyon or peruse the geology exhibits while staying warm and dry.

Rain falling at the rim often evaporates in the dry air before reaching the bottom of the chasm. The South Rim receives an average of 16 inches annually, while the inner gorge gets only 9 inches. This makes a huge difference in the plant life.

The canyon is somewhat like an inverted mountain, but it has its own peculiarities. In the winter, the sun's low angle allows only a few hours of sunlight in the inner depths, but in the summer, it becomes an oven. Exposed rock retains, radiates, and reflects heat contributing to warmer environments in the canyon. At night cold dense air flows over the rim and cools down the air again.

The canyon has four of the world's seven life zones - from Canadian to Lower Sonoran. Elevation plays a critical role in climate and thus plant and animal life. Average temperatures at the river are about 15 degrees warmer than average temperatures at the South Rim.

At lower elevations, the ecosystem changes from ponderosa pines to junipers and pinyon pines. Prickly pear cacti, with flat green pads and yellow and pink flowers, are found below the Supai formation and on the rims along with the broadly distributed spiny cholla. Hopis boiled the yellow fruit of the cholla, often the only vegetable found in March, and so called that month Cactus Moon. Also, some species of cacti begin to bloom during the Cactus Moon month of March.

Sand verbena is one of the flowers tough enough to take the heat along the river; it opens in the evening and gently perfumes the somewhat cooler night air. Moths attracted by the sweet-smelling nectar pollinate the flowers before they close at dawn's early light.

5) Train Depot

The Santa Fe Railway Station looks like a picture from a Lincoln log set. Architect Francis Wilson patterned the Santa Fe Railway Depot after the new El Tovar Hotel in 1909. It was one of about fourteen log depots in the United States. Its unique construction features logs rounded on the outside, but squared on three sides for flat interior walls and flat surfaces between adjoining logs.

The completion of a railroad line from Williams, Arizona was a boon to tourism at the Grand Canyon. The first steam-driven train arrived at Grand Canyon Village on September 17, 1901. Old photos in the rustic log building show a bygone era when the railroad was on the cutting edge of transportation.

As part of their campaign to attract passengers on the Southwest route, Santa Fe Railroad became a major patron of the arts. The company hosted Thomas Moran, William Leigh, Louis Akin, Gunnar Widforss and other artists in exchange for their paintings. They hoped to entice Easterners to ride their railroads and see the wonders of the West. In 1901, one group of artists was led to the rim with eyes closed, so the first view of the canyon would be more dramatic.

Today, the train is a nostalgic, yet convenient, form of transportation. An old locomotive pulls passenger cars on a 56-mile scenic journey between the historic town of Williams and the Grand Canyon. Fully restored 1923 steam engines run from the last weekend in May through September and vintage 1950's diesels run the rest of the year. The train winds its way through scenic pine forests, high desert plains, and small canyons as singing cowboys entertain passengers. Be on the lookout for masked desperados who hold up the train!

6) Hopi House

Since 1905, Hopi House has been a showcase of genuine handcrafted Indian goods. The building itself is a work of art, constructed with the aid of Hopi craftsmen and patterned after the Hopi pueblo of Old Oraibi on Third Mesa.

This trading post was the first of several structures Mary E. J. Colter would design for Fred Harvey. Its blend of commercialism and romanticism came to typify Harvey architecture. The interior displays primitive but effective architecture: massive adobe-like walls of rough plaster, log beam ceilings thatched with layers of saplings, corner fireplaces, and wall niches. Outside, multilevel terraces connect with stone steps and ladders of rough tree limbs.

Upper rooms lodged Indian artisans who worked on their crafts - jewelry, pottery, and blankets - as tourists looked on. Each evening Indians sang traditional songs and danced on the patio.

Although the Indian artisans are no longer in residence, Hopi House is still a wonderful showcase for authentic Native American art and was designated a National Historic Landmark in 1987.

The Hopis live on a small reservation surrounded by the Navajo reservation. Unlike their nomadic neighbors, the Hopis live in villages clustered on top of three mesas. They have inhabited the same villages for more than 900 years, longer than any other community in the United States. Their multi-color basketry, silver overlay jewelry, and pottery are highly prized.

The 20-million acre Navajo Reservation is east of the park. The largest Indian tribe in the United States, the Navajo, are known for fine hand-woven wool rugs and silver jewelry. Some live in traditional eight-sided hogans.

7) El Tovar Hotel

Rocking chairs on wide porches are the first indication of the old-fashioned relaxation and comfort of El Tovar Hotel. Inside the hotel, leather furniture, paintings by Thomas Moran, colorful rugs, and Indian pottery accent the woody interior of the lobby.

The ceiling soars above massive Oregon pine logs, and copper chandeliers hang by chains from the ridgepole while moose and buffalo heads peer down at visitors. Beyond is a rustic but elegant dining room with a massive stone fireplace.

Architect Charles Whittlesey, commissioned by the Santa Fe Railroad, modeled this 100-room hotel to resemble and rival the great European hunting lodges. Completed on January 14, 1905, El Tovar was called "the most expensively constructed and appointed log house in America." Many considered it the most elegant hotel west of the Mississippi. El Tovar was named for a Spanish officer in Coronado's expedition that discovered the canyon while searching for the legendary Seven Golden Cities of Cibola.

El Tovar soon became a mecca for worldly travelers such as playwright George Bernard Shaw; Ferdinand Foch, the Marshal of France; Conductor Arthur Fiedler; Albert Einstein; Western author Zane Grey, and Guglielmo Marconi, radio inventor. President Taft held a dinner party at the hotel in 1909 and Teddy Roosevelt stayed here while hunting cougar in 1913 with the famed lion hunter, Uncle Jim Owen.

Nearly self-sufficient, the hotel had a greenhouse for fresh fruit and vegetables, a chicken house for eggs, and a dairy herd for milk. A coal-fired generator powered electric lights. Water had to be hauled by train daily from 120 miles away. Today water and power are easier to come by and guests can still enjoy the rustic, casual elegance. The rooms were all remodeled and have modern conveniences as well as old-fashioned appeal.

Between El Tovar and the canyon is a bronze plate with a moveable eyepiece to help viewers identify landmarks such as Cheops Pyramid and Zoroaster Temple. Many of the fanciful names, like the Tower of Ra and Isis Temple, refer to Egyptian deities and were given to the canyon's buttes by Clarence Dutton, an early mapmaker with a fascination for temples and thrones who surveyed the northwest canyon in the 1880's.

8) Bright Angel Lodge

Bright Angel Lodge, a pioneer-style log building, has curio shops, restaurants, a lounge, and a cozy lobby with peeled log supports. It is one of the nine buildings in the village included in the National Register of Historic Places. In the History Room is a unique fireplace representing the geology of the canyon. Geologist and park interpreter Edwin McKee selected representative rocks of each layer of the canyon from round river rocks at the base to Kaibab limestone at the top. On each side are large picture windows framing the canyon. Today, the room houses a small Fred Harvey Museum.

Fred Harvey had operated the gift shops, newsstands, restaurants, and hotels of the Atchison, Topeka, and Santa Fe Railway since 1876. In the early days, passengers only had about 20 minutes to find and eat a meal before their train left and Harvey became famous for providing good food and prompt service at reasonable prices. When the Santa Fe Railway purchased a bankrupt Arizona railroad that extended from Williams to copper mines at Anita, they decided to extend the rail line to the South Rim.

Anticipating a large influx of tourists, the Fred Harvey Company built the El Tovar Hotel and staffed it with Harvey girls.

Young, single women were hired by Harvey to provide a high level of service at his establishments. Strict rules maintained Harvey's impeccable standards and protected the Harvey girls and their reputations. In the 1940's, Judy Garland starred in a movie, "The Harvey Girls" which portrayed them as beautiful young maidens dressed in crisply starched uniforms and white aprons. Many came from the East looking for employment and adventure and remained as wives of local ranchers, miners, lumbermen, and railway men. Some say they are the ones who tamed the Wild West.

The Rim Trail on the canyon side of the Bright Angel Lodge is a wonderful place to watch a sunset. The changing angle of the light picks out highpoints and casts them in sharp relief against the deepening shadows. The colors gently mute into pastels of purple, pink, peach, and periwinkle blue. Moreover, if you are lucky and your timing is right, the moon will rise in the east and shed its own luminous light across the monuments of the canyon.

9) Lookout Studio

Built in 1914 and designed by Mary Colter to blend into the landscape rather than dominate it, Lookout Studio clings to the canyon's edge. From a distance, the jagged chimney and native rock of its roof camouflage the building, blending it with canyon walls. Terraces overhanging the chasm offer awe-inspiring perspectives while high-powered telescopes let viewers zoom in on distant canyon features, just as they have since 1914. Grand Canyon Village was once known as Hance's Tank, after Captain John Hance, a trailblazer and renowned yarn-spinner. He was one of the Park's main attractions in the early 20th century, entertaining many visitors including President Theodore Roosevelt.

A visitor once asked, "How did you lose the end of your finger, Captain Hance?" "My finger? Why, ma'am, I wore it off in thirty years of standing here on the rim of the Grand Canyon pointing to the scenery!"

While you are here, look for dark backpack-sized objects on the ledges and you may recognize a California condor or they may be soaring high above you. The magnificent birds have been reintroduced to the Grand Canyon in recent years. They lived near the canyon for thousands of years until pushed to the brink of extinction. The last native Arizona condor sighting was in 1924.

In 1996 and since, a group of the condors has been released north of the Grand Canyon. Until recently, the condors in Arizona were too young to breed. They begin breeding at six or seven years of age and usually lay just one egg, often in a cave. Now there may be a growing number of nests in Arizona.

10) Kolb Studio

Perched on the brink of the Grand Canyon is the photography studio of Emery and Ellsworth Kolb. Beginning in 1902, well before Grand Canyon National Park was founded, the brothers took photos of tourists. Emery boasted that he had, "taken more pictures of men and mules than any other living man."

The nearest water, needed for developing and printing, was at Indian Garden 3,000 feet below in the canyon. Running down the trail past the riders he had just photographed, one of the brothers would develop the glass plates he carried in his pack, then race back up the trail and have the pictures ready at the end of the mule ride.

The Kolbs not only produced many canyon still shots, they were the first to film a Grand Canyon river-running trip in 1911. On a different trip, Emery's daughter Edith was the first woman to brave the Colorado River. Their movie was shown daily until 1975 - the longest running movie in the world. The Kolbs' first darkroom was a small cave with a blanket for a door, but in 1904 the Kolbs built a wood structure. Today, you can pass through the bookstore to the free art and photo gallery shows on the lower floors.

11) Bright Angel Trail Overview

Bright Angel Trail is the most heavily traveled trail down into the canyon because water is available at several locations along the way and it is more gradual in its descent than the South Kaibab, the other popular trail from the South Rim to the Colorado River.

If you decide to go part way down the trail, remember, it takes twice as long to come up as it does to go down. A short hike to the first tunnel will take you past fossils of brachiopods (ancient shelled animals), corals, and sponges that lived in a warm shallow sea two hundred and seventy million years ago. Indian pictographs can be seen to the left and above you after you pass through the tunnel. These were probably left by Havasupai Indians whose descendants live in Havasu Canyon to the west of here.

The mules also take this route, and they have right-of-way. You'll be glad to know you are expected to stand on the INSIDE of the trail, not the outward edge, as they pass by. Of course, if you are riding a mule, you may not like this idea, but mules are sure-footed.

Seeing the canyon between the ears of a mule is an unforgettable experience. In 1902, two famous naturalists, John Muir and John Burroughs, both more than 70 years old, rode the Bright Angel together. The trail was rebuilt after the Park Service took it over in 1928.

When Ferde Grofe traveled down the Bright Angel Trail, he was inspired to write "The Grand Canyon Suite" which included the sound of clip-clopping mules. The music expresses different aspects of the canyon in its five movements: "Sunrise, Painted Desert, On the Trail, Sunset, and Cloudburst." It was featured in Disney's Oscar winning short movie, "Grand Canyon."

12) Trailview Overlook

The Trailview Overlook is an ideal place to look back at the South Rim and the historic buildings of Grand Canyon Village. Beyond them can be seen Red Butte and the San Francisco Peaks. Mount Humphries is the highest point in Arizona, at 12,633 feet. It and the other nearby peaks were part of a larger stratovolcano. Nearby Sunset Crater erupted in 1064 A.D., which is very recent, geologically speaking.

The trail leading away from the village buildings can easily be seen following the Bright Angel Fault down into the canyon along a series of steep switchbacks. A fault is a fracture in the earth's surface, and this one extends across the canyon as do most faults in the Grand Canyon area. Erosion along faults breaks down the canyon walls making side canyons easier places to build trails.

Springs at Indian Garden below have created a small green oasis on the Tonto Platform. Ancestral Puebloans from around A.D. 500-1250 and the Cerbat culture from around A.D. 1300 may have used the water to farm the area and may have hunted bighorn sheep, mule deer, squirrels, and rabbits that were attracted by the water. All of these animal species still live in the canyon - keep an eye out for them!

Prospectors Pete Berry and Ralph Cameron improved an Indian route to Indian Garden in the early 1890's, and Cameron had extended the trail to the river by 1899. The water-loving cottonwood trees at Indian Garden were planted by Ralph Cameron.

Along the stream in late spring and summer, crimson monkey flowers and watercress, an excellent salad and medicinal plant, are found. White showy flowers of the sacred datura plant are also found near Indian Garden. Native Americans sometimes used the narcotic sacred datura to induce visions, but all parts of the plant are poisonous and deadly. Along the Bright Angel Trail pale hop trees and western redbud trees sport magenta blooms in late spring.

The hottest, driest part of the journey is between the Tonto Plateau and the Colorado River where brittle-bush, other desert shrubs, and cacti grow. Hedgehog, claret cup, beavertail, and grizzly-bear cacti love the hot, dry environment. Trailing four-o'clock flowers close up early, by noon in the desert heat. Prickly-poppies bloom when the spring blossoms have faded and the summer flowers are still awaiting the monsoons. One rare poppy species is found only on the steep slopes of the inner canyon.

13) Maricopa Point

Many of the earliest Anglo visitors to the canyon were miners. No gold was found in the canyon, but in 1891 Daniel Lorain Hogan and a Havasupai Indian guide found evidence of copper 1,100 feet below Maricopa Point. Hogan, who was the Flagstaff deputy sheriff and a part-time prospector, filed a 20-acre Orphan Mining claim that included four acres on the rim. To access the claim, he built the Hummingbird Trail, otherwise known as "Hogan's Slide," a precarious trail that included ropes, ladders, and rock steps across the cliff face. He did some mining but rarely shipped any copper. Later, Hogan was one of Teddy Roosevelt's Rough Riders and served in the Spanish American War in 1898.

President Teddy Roosevelt signed the papers that converted the claim to private property in 1906. In 1936, Hogan opened a tourist facility on the site that eventually consisted of twenty cabins, a trading post, curio shops, and a saloon.

In 1951, amateur prospectors discovered that the worthless gray rock found with the copper ore was radioactive - some of the richest uranium ore in the Southwest. From 1956 to 1969, half a million tons of Grand Canyon uranium ore was hauled to Tuba City for processing, fueling the nation's atomic energy program.

While the copper mine had only one short horizontal tunnel, the uranium mine was a complex underground network of shafts and chambers. The towering head frame of the Orphan Mine is still visible. The last shipment left the park on April 25, 1969 as demand for uranium had declined.

In the late 1960's, the property owners came up with a new moneymaking idea - a multistory hotel. It would cascade down the canyon's edge below Maricopa Point "like a waterfall." While some people thought this more of a blackmail scheme to get Congress to purchase the claim, Congress decided to purchase the property and it became a part of the National Park in 1987, without the cascading hotel.

14) Powell Point

An impressive monument was erected at Powell Point in 1915 honoring John Wesley Powell and his party. They were the first people to run the Colorado River through the Grand Canyon in August 1869 and again in September 1872. Since so little was known about the river and its rapids, the group was truly taking a plunge into the unknown. Powell wrote, "With some feeling of anxiety, we enter a new canyon this morning. We have learned to closely observe the texture of the rock. In softer strata, we have a quiet river; in harder, we find rapids and falls. Below us are the limestone and hard sandstones . . . This bodes toil and danger."

In fact, one crewmember, Frank Goodman, left after experiencing the first rapid way back in northern Utah. Hundreds of miles further downstream, brothers Oramel and Seneca Howland, as well as William Dunn, decided they would rather take their chances with the Indians and a steep climb out than run the rest of the river. That decision cost them their lives. Their names do not appear on the monument because some considered them deserters.

Powell was a self-taught scientist and major of artillery who lost his right arm in the Civil War. He aimed, "to add a mite to the great sum of human knowledge" as his group started out from Green River, Wyoming in 1869 with four wooden boats. Three months later, they emerged from the canyon at Grand Wash Cliffs with only two battered boats and missing much of their equipment.

On both trips, Powell and his men made detailed drawings and notes on the geology, flora, fauna, and Indian ruins of the canyon. They mapped and named many of the formations and features of the canyon. Silver Creek, later named Bright Angel Creek, received its name because its clear water was such a contrast to the muddy water of "Dirty Devil," a stream the river rafters had encountered earlier in their journey. Powell popularized the name "Grand Canyon" and many attribute his descriptions of the region in *Canyons of the Colorado* for putting the canyon on the map as a "must see" - the beginning of the tourism boom.

15) Hopi Point

Hopi Point projects further out into the canyon than others, affording vistas in all directions. As the Fred Harvey Company advertised, "the panorama here, in broad daylight, seems to be the acme of scenic beauty. But when the afternoon sun . . . gradually sinks beneath the far mountain ranges, banked with clouds . . . the canyon depths become a world of mystery, with giant forms dimly outlined in the ghostly void. And then, miracle of miracles! The western sky becomes a riot of vivid colors, flaming across a field of turquoise, and fading to the afterglow."

A bronze plaque at Hopi Point commemorates the men of the Civilian Conservation Corps or CCC, sometimes known as "Roosevelt's Tree Army." During the Depression of the 1930's, many young men were unemployed. The CCC, Roosevelt's most popular New Deal program, put young men to work in national forests, national parks and state parks.

"Save the soil, save the forest, save the young men," was one of their slogans. By the end of the CCC program in 1942, more than 3,000,000 had enrolled and worked in over 4,500 locations.

The first CCC group arrived at the Grand Canyon on May 29, 1933. Participants signed up for six months at $30 a month of which $25 was sent to the man's family. Eight hundred men constructed roads, overlooks, fences, trails, rest houses, telephone lines, rock walls, buildings, picnic shelters, campgrounds and bridges. In this way, many of the men learned a trade. A sense of pride replaced hopelessness. Their unofficial motto became "We Can Take It." And, as one young man said, "It was the greatest thing that ever happened to me." Many amenities created by the CCC are still enjoyed by park visitors today.

16) Mohave Point

Mohave Point is a good place to view and contemplate the Colorado River. Although the river appears only a few feet wide from this height, its width ranges from 76 to 300 feet. Three rapids are visible below in Granite Gorge: Salt Creek, Granite, and Hermit. Hermit Rapid and many other canyon features were named for the prospector and tourist guide, Louis Boucher, who lived a solitary life in the side canyons from 1889 to 1912.

The Colorado River starts as trickles of glacier water high in the Colorado Rockies and Wind River Range of Wyoming. At 1450 miles in length, it is one of America's longest rivers. In the first 237 miles of the 277-mile-long Grand Canyon, it drops almost 2,000 feet, an average of 8 feet per mile. The flow, which can be as much as 25 miles per hour, sweeps away bits of the canyon walls as they are loosened by rain, to be carried downward by gravity, streams, and wind. Before Glen Canyon Dam was built upriver, the river carried away about 500,000 tons of sand, mud and dissolved minerals per day.

During storms and high water, the force of the water can carry bigger loads and the deafening sound of rolling rocks and crashing boulders is a mere hint of the river's power. Eventually, the Colorado reaches the Gulf of California. By then, all of its water has been siphoned off to supply drinking water for cities in Nevada, California, and Arizona plus irrigation water for both the U.S. and Mexico.

A sand-dune environment along the river is home to cacti, yucca and lizards such as the western whiptail, chuckwallas, desert collared lizards and the pink Grand Canyon rattlesnake.

The combination of the river, the changes in elevation, and the width of the canyon have separated members of some species such as the mountain lion, spotted skunk, cliff chipmunk and common pocket gopher, so that over time they have evolved into separate subspecies on each rim. For instance, the Kaibab tassel-eared squirrel is found only on the North Rim. With a dark body and white tail; it has evolved differently than its relative, the Abert squirrel of the South Rim which also has tufted ears, but a smaller, red-brown body, and gray tail. Here in the canyon, the interaction between environment, plants, and animals is obvious and striking.

17) The Abyss

At the Abyss waypoint, you are standing at the edge of the Mohave Wall, a 3,000-foot sheer drop to the Tonto Platform. This is a good place to look at the rainbow of layers in the cliffs; each one has a story to tell about the environment at a certain period of time.

In the deepest inner gorge, igneous granite intrusions squeezed up into fissures in the basement rocks such as the Vishnu schist metamorphic rocks. Some of these rocks are as old as 1800 million years and form the basement of the North American continent.

The next layer is lavender-brown Tapeats Sandstone, the base of the gently sloping Tonto Platform. It was deposited as coastal sand dunes and in shallow coastal waters near the edge of the Tapeats Sea. Greenish Bright Angel Shale above the Tapeats Sandstone was formed from mud that was deposited as the sea level rose. In it are traces of shells, seaweed, worms, and trilobites. Since shale erodes easily, it forms the broad Tonto Platform atop the harder Tapeats.

The steep cliff of the Redwall Limestone is not really red, at least not all the way through. Originally blue-gray, it was stained by rainwater flowing down through the overlying Supai and Hermit Redbeds. Abundant fossils of brachiopids, bryozoans, and other critters of a warm, shallow, clear-water ocean are found in the Redwall limestone. The fossil rings which look like the disks of a candy necklace were once part of the long flexible stalk of a crinoid, a sea lily.

Oxidized iron creates the red color in the Supai Group, which was deposited in environments that varied from rivers and deltas to coastal beach dunes to shallow seas. In the bright red Hermit Shale above the Supai, ripple marks, rain dimples, and mud cracks have been preserved, as well as fossils of plants, amphibians, and reptiles.

If you looked through a microscope, the individual grains of sand in rocks formed in beach environments are rounded and polished in appearance. The individual grains of sand in the yellow cliffs of the Coconino Sandstone, however, are much different. They are angular and so criss-crossed with scratches that they appear frosted, like little bits of broken glass. These grains were deposited as sand dunes in a Sahara-like sand sea that extended northward as far as today's Montana about 275 million years ago. Tracks, but no bones, of small reptiles have been found here.

This area then went through more changes as the seas advanced across the land again creating the Toroweap Formation. Its tan sandstones and limestones are layered with lighter colored gypsum. Brachiopods, mollusks, corals, and bryozoans are in these beds. In the canyon today, the Toroweap Formation is the slope with trees and bushes between the distinctive cliffs of Coconino Sandstone and Kaibab Limestone.

The top layer of the rim is gray and creamy-colored Kaibab Limestone, from 270 million years ago. It tells us that once again a shallow sea covered this spot. The seas go in and the seas go out. Do you see the fossils beneath your feet that were left behind?

18) Pima Point

The Colorado River is 4,400 feet below Pima Point, but on a still day you can hear the water as it rushes through Granite and Boucher Rapids. More than 50 miles to the northwest is Mt. Trumball, the highest peak in a cluster of now-dormant cinder cones and volcanoes on the Uinkaret Plateau. About a million years ago, lava flows from there cascaded over the rim of the canyon and dammed the river. One flowed down the riverbed over 80 miles.

When Powell floated through the canyon, he observed, "A cinder cone, or extinct volcano, stands on the very brink of the canyon. What a conflict of water and fire there must have been here! Just imagine a river of molten rock running down into a river of melted snow. What a seething and boiling of the waters, what clouds of steam rolled into the heavens!"

For many years, visitors could stay at Hermit Camp, built below this point on the Tonto Platform. They had to hike or ride a mule down, but their supplies were sent down a 6,000-foot tramway. The seven-eighths inch steel cable plummeted over the rim and down to the camp without any intermediate supports. It was the longest single-span tram in the world. Of course, a few daring employees and village residents also had to try the quick way down - a terrifying 20-minute joyride over the edge.

The Hermit Camp was built by the Santa Fe Railroad in 1912 to compete with camps operated by William Bass, Ralph Cameron, and David Rust. It offered "camping out deluxe:" Eleven tent cabins accommodated 30 people with "restful beds, rugs and other conveniences." Guests ate well at the central dining hall with meals prepared by a Fred Harvey chef. Amenities included phones, showers, restrooms, stables, and a blacksmith's shop. For entertainment, guests could hike along Hermit Creek to the river or ride the Tonto Trail. The camp was abandoned in 1930 and the tram was dismantled. Sorry, no more joyrides over the edge.

19) Hermits Rest

The first sight you see at Hermits Rest is an arch of carelessly piled stones with a broken mission bell. In earlier days, a lantern hung from a projecting stone to guide weary travelers. Beyond is a stone building that looks like it grew from the land. Although it appears to be a haphazard jumble of stones with a chimney, it was carefully designed by Mary Colter, one of the first women architects, to blend with, not distract from, the canyon.

Inside, the focal point is a massive vaulted fireplace. After it was completed in 1914, someone asked Colter, "Why don't you clean up this place?" She laughingly replied, "You can't imagine what it cost to make it look this old." Hand-hewn posts support the large log beams of the front porch and a low stone wall extends to the rim where an historic viewfinder offers close-up views of the river. You are likely to encounter a highly intelligent raven that mimics a wide variety of animal and people voices or a rock squirrel looking for fallen tidbits.

Hermits Rest is the end of the line for the free shuttle bus service and the Rim Trail, but Hermits Trail continues from here. Rated very strenuous, it descends for 8.9 miles to the Colorado River at Hermit Rapid.

Even a short trek into the depths of the canyon will give you a different perspective, however. Fossils of sponges and corals are seen on the way down to the Coconino Sandstone. In the sandstone you can see tracks of animals that climbed and slipped down the dunes 275 million years ago. Look for them on a large slab of rock about two thirds of the way through a well-cobbled section of the trail known as the White Zig-Zags. You won't see any dinosaur tracks or bones in the canyon because those rock layers have been eroded away in this region. They have been found, however, in the Painted Desert and the Petrified Forest National Parks in Arizona.

The junction with Waldron Trail is a good turn-around point. Each time you pause to catch your breath on the way back up the trail, you can enjoy a different panoramic view of the canyon. Early spring wildflowers can be incredibly diverse, if winter brought enough moisture. Just below the rim, white blossoms cover fendlerbush and serviceberry shrubs. The pale-yellow desert brickellbush and golden yellow stick-leaf flowers are also common. It's well worth the hike.

20) South Kaibab Trail Overview

Are you ready to hike rim to rim? You'll need a backcountry permit and a strong heart and legs. The South Kaibab Trail drops almost 5,000 feet to the river in less than seven miles with scenic picture spots, but no water sources until you reach the river and no clean water until you reach Bright Angel Campground. In this desert environment, strong, erosion-resistant rocks like limestone form cliffs, and weaker rocks like shale form slopes.

A series of switchbacks take you through the Kaibab and Red Wall Limestones, but the trail also follows long, red Cedar Ridge beneath O'Neil Butte and levels out again before plunging into the inner gorge at the "Tipoff." The trail disappears into a narrow tunnel and emerges on the far side at a bridge with solid wood flooring and screened sides. Mules won't cross a bridge if they can see moving water beneath their feet. On the far side, the trail continues along the river, past an ancient Indian dwelling and leads to Phantom Ranch.

After World War I, Fred Harvey built Phantom Ranch for guests who took his mule trips into the canyon. The buildings were built with large, round river rocks from the area while all other material had to be brought in by mule. Facilities included several individual cabins, a large dining hall and a recreation hall. In the 1930's, the Civilian Conservation Corps added a swimming pool and constructed the River Trail connecting the Bright Angel and South Kaibab Trails on the south side of the river.

Locoweed flowers, which are addictive and deadly to grazers like horses and cattle, bloom in February and March on the river beaches. Of course, some people say those rim-to-rim hikers are pretty loco too. The 14-mile North Kaibab Trail continues along Bright Angel Creek and then climbs to the North Rim. It generally takes twice as long to hike out to the North Rim as it does to hike in from the South, and that was all downhill.

21) Yaki Point

The North Rim is 1,000 feet higher than the South Rim - high enough to get six to ten feet of snow and support forests of aspen, spruce, and fir. Living in the forest are mule deer, mountain lions, porcupines, red squirrels, and Kaibab squirrels. Birds include turkeys, great horned owls, saw-whet owls, broad-tailed hummingbirds, hairy woodpeckers, hermit thrushes, Clark's nutcrackers, Steller's jays, and mountain bluebirds.

On the South Rim, tall ponderosa pines are found in washes and protected areas with deeper soil, along with Gambel oak, fernbush, and grasses. Most of the animals of the spruce-fir forest are also found here. More extensive on the South Rim is the pinyon-juniper forest which thrives with rain from summer monsoon thunderstorms and light winter snows. Coyotes, gray foxes, desert cottontail rabbits, rock squirrels, and cliff chipmunks live here, along with various lizards and snakes. Flitting among the trees are pinyon and scrub jays, mourning doves, plain titmice, Bewick's wrens, gray-throated warblers, juncos, and nuthatches.

The number and size of trees diminishes below the Rim, but agave, desert thorn, Mormon tea, cacti, and yucca thrive. Indians ate the fruit of the banana yucca raw, roasted it, dried it for winter use, ground it into meal, and fermented it into an alcoholic drink. From the leaves, they had fiber for rope, mats, sandals, baskets, and cloth. From the roots, they made soap and laxatives. Tall, showy golden prince's-plume is seen on steep rock slopes throughout much of the year. Occasionally seen are bighorn sheep, black-tailed jackrabbits, spotted skunks, antelope, ground squirrels, and desert woodrats.

Along the Colorado River is a narrow corridor of the Mohave Desert where cacti and low shrubs grow. The Utah agave is also found here, as well as in many other parts of the park. Agaves are often called century plants because many years pass before their once-in-a-lifetime flowering stalk appears.

22) Grandview Point

After a 75-mile ride from Flagstaff on a dusty, jolting stage-coach, guests were glad to see the three-story Grandview Hotel with dormer windows that once stood at this location. Then, as one 19th-century visitor reported, they were awed to walk around the corner of the large log hotel and see the immense canyon stretched out below them with shadows and sunlight highlighting the myriad buttes and cliffs. The front porch was supported by stalagmites and stalactites from a cave in the canyon. The inside was rustic but comfortable with Indian rugs and rocking chairs near a large fireplace.

The owner and builder of the hotel was a former saloonkeeper from Flagstaff, Peter D. Berry. He often prospected in the canyon with only a pack burro for company until one lucky day in 1892 when he came across a copper deposit. The ore was up to 70% pure - so rich that it was exhibited at Chicago's World Fair in 1893. He worked hard at the mine, but it was a tough way to earn a living, hauling ore up 2,600 vertical feet!

Berry discovered that he could make more money as a guide and with the hotel than with his Last Chance Mine. When the railroad line was extended and hotels were built 13 miles to the west, his business took a dive. Eventually, the Grandview was sold to William Randolph Hearst who used it as a vacation retreat for family and friends in the early 1900's.

The four mile Grandview Trail was originally Pete Berry's trail to the mine down on Horseshoe Mesa, the top of the Redwall Formation. In some places along the cliff, the trail consisted of logs anchored to the wall with chains which are now gone. It is still a steep and narrow trail but the top part is shaded by pines and has impressive views. Down on Horseshoe Mesa, a couple of mine openings can still be seen along with a roofless stone building. The mine, the hotel, and the guides are gone, but their names and their legacy linger on at the canyon.

23) Moran Point

Moran Point is named for Thomas Moran who spent nearly every winter at the Grand Canyon from 1899 to 1920 and created some of the most widely recognized paintings of the canyon. Moran's paintings were influential in convincing President Theodore Roosevelt to declare the site a national monument. "The Chasm of the Colorado" was inspired by the view from Point Sublime on the North Rim and was painted as a companion piece to "The Grand Canyon of the Yellowstone", the first landscape by an American artist to hang in the U.S. Capitol in Washington, D.C.

The first artists accompanied surveyors and explorers. On the second Powell trip in 1871, seventeen-year-old Frederick Samuel Dellenbaugh sketched views all along the river and painted a canyon view in 1875. Also on the Powell journey was John Hillers who took the first photos of the River. Ansel Adams may be one of the best-known artists who have captured canyon views on film.

Artists have come from all over the world to capture the canyon's beauty. Heinrich Baldwin Mollhausen made about 130 sketches of the area in the 1850's. Sadly, a fire in Berlin destroyed all but six during World War II. Because of his colorful description of the expedition, Mollhausen was sometimes called the German James Fenimore Cooper.

Several artists lived at the canyon including Warren Rollins, Widforss, and Louis Akin. Bruce Aiken was employed by the National Park Service to tend the park's water source at Roaring Springs. He and his wife raised three children below the Rim. His artwork reflects his intimate and long-term relationship with the canyon.

Portraying the canyon with words may be even harder than doing it with paint, yet many books have been written about it. Some of the most fascinating are by early explorers such as Francisco Tomas Garces who wrote *A Record of Travel in Arizona and California, 1775-1776.* A more recent explorer was Colin Fletcher, the first man to walk the entire length of the canyon. He wrote about his experiences in *The Man Who Walked Through Time.*

A perennial favorite is a children's book about a prospector's burro, *Brighty of the Grand Canyon* by Marguerite Henry. The spunky little burro was so popular that a statue of Brighty sits in the Grand Canyon Lodge on the North Rim and a movie was made from the book.

A popular songwriter of the early 1900's, Alfred Bryan was inspired to write a poem about nature's rock music: "I am the Grand Canyon . . . I am a dissonance of aeons crashing their epochs in countless Illiads of eternity. I am the wild music of the Valkyries, halted in the Heavens and hushed into stone."

Many artists have tried to capture the grandeur of the canyon through painting, photography, prose, poetry, and music. It's not easy. One artist, William R. Leigh, complained: "What a wretched makeshift these paltry pigments. How hopeless to attempt; what inconceivable impudence to dream of imitating anything so ineffable! It challenges man's utmost skill; it mocks and defies his puny efforts to grasp and perpetuate, through art, its inimitable grandeur."

Gustave Baumann called the canyon an 'artist's nightmare'. He lamented, "You see a wonderful composition and when you look back, it's gone. See how fast the clouds are moving. This is the reason nobody can paint the canyon." Fortunately, artists keep trying, and the results can be magnificent.

24) Tusayan Ruin

Against the vast expanse of time represented by the rocks of the canyon, man's existence has been brief. A former Grand Canyon Park Naturalist, Merrill D. Beal, in his booklet *Grand Canyon - The Story Behind the Scenery*, translated the canyon's millions of years into a timescale more people will understand - a 24-hour day starting at midnight.

As a very general estimate, the rocks of the inner canyon formed a bit after 2:00 P.M. and the river doesn't begin to carve the Grand Canyon until after 11:58 P.M. The first humans on the North American continent show up about a quarter of a second before midnight.

On a human scale, the traces of human habitation in the canyon are very old. It is believed that up to ten to twelve thousand years ago, hunter-gatherer people were roaming the canyon looking for food as archaeologists have found Clovis and Folsom stone spear points in the canyon area. Deep within canyon caves, they discovered little toy-like figures made of split twigs twisted into effigies of deer and mountain sheep. Some are pierced by tiny spears. This civilization apparently left the canyon about 1000 B.C. No signs of human habitation have been discovered from the next 1,500 years.

Then, around 500 A.D. came the ancestral Puebloan or basketmaker people as they were known because of their fine baskets and woven sandals. They hunted deer, bighorn sheep, rabbit, and other animals while gathering pinyon nuts, agave, and local plant materials.

By 1050 A.D., pueblo farmers had built communities on both the river deltas and the rim. With the seasons, they alternated between the low and high areas to stretch their growing season. They adapted new farming techniques such as check dams and terraces, crafted elegant pottery, developed bows and throwing sticks and lived in above-ground masonry villages. Two thousand sites have been found. Around 1250 A.D. these Indians disappeared, perhaps because of a severe drought. They may have relocated to the Hopi Mesa area of northeastern Arizona, where the oldest settlements date to this time or may have moved on to the Rio Grande River Valley.

The Tusayan Ruin were built around 1200 A.D. The pueblo has living spaces, storage rooms, and a kiva, a ceremonial gathering place, for about 30 people. Archaeologists believe two generations lived here. The stone and masonry interpretive center was completed in 1932 and named the MacCurdy Wayside Museum of Archeology in honor of the woman who donated the money to build it. Today, this is known as the Tusayan Museum.

25) Lipan Point

Although Native Americans roamed the canyon for thousands of years, Anglos did not come upon it until 1540, and it would be many more years before they reached the river.

Francisco Vasquez Coronado was not looking for scenic sites when he came through the area in 1540. He was looking for gold in the Seven Cities of Cibola. Hopi Indians told one of his officers, Pedro de Tovar, about a great river twenty day's journey west of their village. Hoping that it might be the long-sought Northwest Passage, Coronado sent Garcia de Cardenas and twelve men on an exploratory mission. From the top of the Coconino Plateau, they could see a thin thread of water far below. Their Indian guides advised them not to try to reach the river, but three of the men tried to climb down to it. They reported that the buttes and towers which "appeared from above to be the height of a man, were higher than the tower of the Cathedral of Seville." The Spaniards gave up and Cardenas reported to Coronado that the river was of no use to them.

Two hundred years later, another Spaniard, Father Francisco Tomas Garces, descended into the western end of the canyon and visited the Havasupai Indians. Because the great river was thick with red mud, he called it Colorado, Spanish for red.

Captain Lorenzo Sitgreaves was instructed in 1851 to follow the Colorado River to the Gulf of California because the United States Government was hoping to find a river route to the West Coast. He tried, but had to turn southwest at the Grand Falls of the Little Colorado because the proposed route was "too hazardous."

Lieutenant Joseph Christmas Ives maneuvered his boat up to Black Canyon near today's Boulder Dam and then went cross-country until returning to the river at Diamond Creek. Ives was looking for a navigable river, so despite his awe, he assayed the canyon as "altogether valueless" . . . "It can be approached only from the south and after entering it there is nothing to do but leave. Ours has been the first and will doubtless be the last party of whites to visit this profitless locality."

Powell turned the tide of opinion as described at Powell Point. Now, people sign up months in advance for raft trips through the Grand Canyon, ranging from mild to wild rides including class 10 rapids! Visitors come away with an increased appreciation of the river and the canyon.

But, just to show that you still can't please everybody, one modern-day tourist dismissed the canyon as "Nothing but a bad case of erosion," and a cowboy once remarked, "It'd be a helluva place to lose a cow."

26) Navajo Point

Like several other waypoints along the South Rim, Navajo Point is named for a Southwestern Indian tribe. There are many different Indian tribes that have a special connection to the Grand Canyon including Navajo, Havasupai, Hopi, Hualapai, Paiute, Zuni, Apache, and three groups of Paiute. Many have legends depicting the origin of their people connected to the Grand Canyon.

The largest Native American reservation in the United States belongs to the Navajo and includes Canyon De Chelly National Monument, Navajo National Monument, Monument Valley Tribal Park, Canyon del Muerto, the south shore of Lake Powell and Rainbow Bridge. The Navajo reservation borders on the eastern edge of the Grand Canyon with excellent views of the Little Colorado River from the trading post at Cameron. Roadside vendors of native crafts also offer many opportunities to take a bit of the southwest home with you.

The Hualapai, "Pine Tree People," have a million-acre reservation west of the National Park that extends for 110 miles along the South Rim. In the 1860's, Chief Wauba-Yuba led the Hualapai in a brief but furious battle. U.S. Government troops defeated them in 1886 however, and they yielded their aboriginal lands to settlers, miners, and ranchers. After a few years, they were allowed to return to their land and have lived there ever since, mainly as ranchers.

Their cousins, the Havasupai, "People of the Blue-green Water", live and farm in Havasu Canyon, a beautiful, photogenic side canyon with travertine pools and waterfalls accessible only by hiking or helicopter. They consider themselves guardians of the canyon and are allowed to use some of the National Park lands for traditional activities such as gathering.

Paiute Indians were hunter-gatherers who made seasonal trips to the North Rim. They lived in brush shelters and spent summers on the Kaibab Plateau and other high country, then moved to lower elevations for the winter. Today, a small band lives on the Kaibab Reservation in far northern Arizona. The San Juan Southern Piaute and Piaute Indian Tribe of Utah also maintain their connections to the Grand Canyon.

The canyon is also important to the Hopi people. "Far down in the lowest depths of the Canyon of the Little Colorado River, at the place where we used to gather salt, is the Sipapu where we emerged from the underworld. All people came up from the below at that place," says an old legend. The circular spring is the Sipapu or doorway to the underworld. The entrance through the roof of a Hopi kiva, an underground room used for ceremonies, symbolizes the Sipapu.

One Hopi legend tells of Tiyo, a Hopi youth who wanted to discover where the waters of the River went. In a box made from a hollow cottonwood tree, he rode through the rapids, fell over waterfalls, and spun through whirlpools until he landed on a muddy bank. He heard a sound from a small round hole, the home of Spider-Woman who weaves the clouds to bring rain. She invited him into her home. Spider-Woman taught him the ceremonies still performed by the Hopis. After many wonderful adventures, Tiyo was lifted from the underworld, along with two beautiful maidens who took him home. Tiyo and his brother married the maidens, and their descendents, two clans of the Hopi, still perform the ceremonies to produce rain in the desert.

27) Desert View

The canyon opens up at Desert View to reveal distant views of the Vermilion Cliffs, San Francisco Peaks, the Painted Desert, and the Colorado River. The views are even better from the 70-foot round stone tower.

Its designer, Mary Elizabeth Jane Colter, was a schoolteacher from St. Paul, Minnesota with an education in architecture and design, until Fred Harvey offered her a job in 1902. During her 40-year association with the Harvey Company and the Santa Fe Railroad, she acted as architect, designer, and decorator. She embraced a new style of architecture with structures that seemed to grow out of the land and reflected the cultural heritage of the region rather than imitating European styles.

The distinctive Watchtower was designed as a re-creation of Ancestral Puebloan structures in the Four Corners region. Scholars debate if the original towers were built as lookouts or for ceremonial purposes, such as those preserved at Toroweep National Monument. This tower has elements of both.

Adorning the walls are images from the myths of the Hopi. Windows allow views in all directions. At the top of the first flight of steps, a door leads to a rooftop viewing platform. The top floor has large windows with views of the Colorado as it makes a grand turn and enters into the inner gorge.

The mighty Colorado River flows in via Utah, from sources in Colorado's Rocky Mountains and Wyoming's Wind River Range. Just east of here, it joins with the Little Colorado River which has its origins in the White Mountains of Arizona. Although much debated, a widely accepted theory is that the canyon is the result of headward erosion by a river that drained off the southwest corner of the Colorado Plateau. It worked its way eastward across the plateau eventually intercepting and capturing the ancestral Colorado River.

It's something to think about as you look back into the Grand Canyon and out over the beautiful vistas to the east. From the ancestral Puebloans to modern day men and women, the Grand Canyon has an irresistible pull to come, to see, to explore, and … to wonder … to be in awe of the Power that created it.

28) Grand Canyon North Rim

One of the most common questions in Arizona is "Which side of the Grand Canyon is better, the South Rim or North Rim?" Like most comparative debates, this one is best answered with "It depends ..." If some cell coverage, IMAX theaters, warm temperatures, and proximity to interstates are a must, then the South Rim is for you. However, if you are looking to get away from the crowds and prefer conifers to cactus, the North Rim is your kind of paradise.

Getting to the North Rim is not easy. For most of the year, deep snow makes it inaccessible to all but the most athletic backcountry skiers. Even when the road is open between late May and early October, the North Rim is fully three hours farther away from Las Vegas, Nevada or Phoenix, Arizona than the South Rim.

However, when looking down from the forested vantage of the North Rim, the canyon's tremendous story of erosion looks less like devastation and more like craftsmanship.

Seeing the Grand Canyon as both a production and destruction leads to a more enlightened understanding and appreciation of this world wonder. Indeed, just a big-hole-in-the-ground thinking is like accusing Michelangelo of defacing blocks of marble.

Theodore Roosevelt understood the canyon's duality. When proclaiming it a national monument in 1908, Roosevelt called it, "the most impressive piece of scenery I have ever looked at. It is beautiful and terrible and unearthly." Although Roosevelt spoke from the South Rim, if he were alive today, he would undoubtedly be a "north-rimmer". Speaking just as directly to untold future generations as he was the tourism developers in attendance, Roosevelt concluded his speech in 1903 with a poignant caution, "Leave it as it is! You cannot improve upon it! The ages have been at work on it, and man can only mar it."

While a cynic, standing at the South Rim could grumble that Roosevelt's admonition was forgotten long ago, an optimist should take the cynic by the hand and say, "Roosevelt's Grand Canyon still exists! We just need to go to the North Rim."

Waypoint Tours®

Plan, Enhance & Cherish
Your Travel Adventures!

This Waypoint Tour® is your
personal tour guide unlocking the
fascinating highlights, history,
geology & nature of
Grand Canyon National Park.

Waypoint Tours® are entertaining,
educational, self-guided tours to help
plan your travel adventures,
enhance your travel experience &
cherish your travel memories.

Travel Destinations include:
Alaska Mt. McKinley Denali AK
Bryce Canyon UT
Grand Canyon South Rim AZ
Grand Canyon North Rim AZ
Grand Teton WY
Rocky Mountains CO
San Antonio & Missions TX
San Diego CA
San Francisco CA
Sedona Red Rock Country AZ
Washington DC
Yellowstone WY
Yosemite CA
Zion UT

Tour Guide Books Plus DVD & MP3s
Tour Road Guides Plus Audio CDs
Tour Guide Books
GPS Waypoint Tours® for iPhones +
DVD & CD Complete Tour Packages
DVD Tour Guides
DVD Tour Postcards
MP3 Downloadable Audio Tours

Waypoint Tours® Available at:
www.waypointtours.com
www.amazon.com
www.itunes.com

Highlights, History, Geology,
Nature & More!

Credits

Book by Waypoint Tours®
Photography by Waypoint Tours®
Original Tour Script by Bonnie Kline
Editing & Writing by Laurie Ann
Maps by the National Park Service

Special thanks to the
Grand Canyon Association & the
Grand Canyon National Park Service.
Support Grand Canyon National Park
with a membership or donation to:

Grand Canyon Association
P.O. Box 399
Grand Canyon, AZ 86023
(928) 638-2481
www.grandcanyon.org

Grand Canyon National Park Service
P.O. Box 129
Grand Canyon, AZ 86023
(928) 638-7888
www.nps.gov/grca

Photo Credits:
*All historic photographs are courtesy of the
Grand Canyon National Park Museum
Collection, image numbers as follows:
Page 23: 09654B. 34: 11344. Page 36:
17234. Page 43: 09944. Page 44: 08437.
Page 49L: 06255. Page 51B: 12005. Page
58: 16942.
Pages(by) 9T, 10T, 13B(Mike Quinn), 14T,
16TB, 19B(Mark Lellouch), 24, 25B, 26B,
45T, 46, 47T(Michael Anderson), 47B, 55B,
60T, 61T(Mike Quinn)
by the National Park Service
Pages 30, 37B(unedited) by Erika Strom
T=Top, B=Bottom, R=Right, L=Left
Printed in China*

Optional Audio CD Contents

Audio CD Driving Tour (75 min)

Optional DVD-ROM Contents

DVD Narrated Tour (45 min)
MP3 Audio Tour (75 min)
PC Multimedia Screensaver
Digital Photo Gallery

Breathtaking Photography,
Professional Narration &
Beautiful Orchestration

DVD Plays Worldwide in All Regions
DVD Mastered in HD in English
* Denotes Waypoints on DVD Video
PC Multimedia Screensaver &
Digital Photo Gallery Each Contain
80+ High-Resolution Photos

Professional Voicing by
Janet Ault & Mark Andrews
Recording Studio at Audiomakers
For private non-commercial use only
Detailed info & credits on
DVD-ROM

Optional CD & DVD-ROM Info

Track #) Title

Grand Canyon Village Area Tour
1) Grand Canyon South Rim*
2) Mather Point*
3) Canyon View Information Plaza*
4) Yavapai Point*
5) Train Depot*
6) Hopi House
7) El Tovar Hotel*
8) Bright Angel Lodge*
9) Lookout Studio*
10) Kolb Studio
11) Bright Angel Trail Overview*

Western Hermit Road Tour
12) Trailview Overlook*
13) Maricopa Point*
14) Powell Point*
15) Hopi Point
16) Mohave Point
17) The Abyss
18) Pima Point*
19) Hermits Rest*

Eastern Desert View Drive Tour
20) South Kaibab Trail Overview*
21) Yaki Point
22) Grandview Point
23) Moran Point
24) Tusayan Ruin
25) Lipan Point*
26) Navajo Point
27) Desert View*

Leave No Trace